SUNDIATA
A LEGEND OF AFRICA
THE LION OF MALI

ADAPTED BY
Will Eisner

NANTIER · BEALL · MINOUSTCHINE
Publishing inc.
new york

SUNDIATA

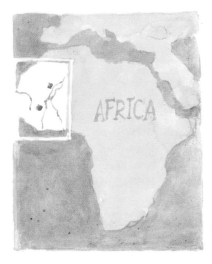

Early in the thirteenth century, the people living along the Senegal River in West Africa were subjugated by a powerful King of Sosso who was reputed to have great magical powers. His name was Sumanguru and he expanded his conquest by defeating the nation of Mali which had been founded by the salt and gold trading Malinke people on the Niger River south of Koumbi Saleh.

After years of Sumanguru's cruel oppression, there arose a young Mali prince named Sundiata who led an army of his people that succeeded in defeating the evil Sumanguru.

The great battle that took place in Kirine became famous as a struggle against a villain who had great magic at his command. It resulted in a stunning defeat of Sumanguru by the people of Mali. This gave rise to the many legends of SUNDIATA that were orally narrated by "griot" storytellers down the years.

Historians tell us that there are some 30 versions of this saga. This is yet another.

Other adaptations by Will Eisner:
Moby Dick, $15.95 hc, $7.95 pb
The Princess & the Frog, $15.95 hc
The Last Knight, $15.95 hc, $7.95 pb
Other adaptations:
The Wind in the Willows, vols. 1-4, $15.95 each
The Fairy Tales of Oscar Wilde, vols. 1-3, $15.95 each
The Jungle Book, $16.95
Fairy Tales of the Brothers Grimm, $15.95
Peter & The Wolf, $15.95
($3 P&H 1st item, $1 each addt'l)

We have over 150 graphic novels in
stock, ask for our color catalog:
NBM, dept. S
555 8th Ave., Suite 1202
New York, NY 10018
www.nbmpublishing.com/tales

ISBN 1-56163-332-1, clothbound
ISBN 1-56163-340-2, paperback
© 2002 Will Eisner
printed in Hong Kong

5   4   3   2   1

Library of Congress Cataloging-in-Publication Data
Eisner, Will.
   Sundiata : a legend of Africa / Will Eisner.
      p. cm.
   Summary: A retelling in comic strip form of the African epic in which an ugly, crippled child grows up to become the liberator and founder of the great empire of old Mali.
   ISBN 1-56163-332-1 -- ISBN 1-56163-340-2 (pbk.)
   1. Keita, Soundiata, d. 1255--Legends. [1. Keita, Soundiata, d. 1255--Cartoons and comics. 2. Mandingo (African people)--Folklore. 3. Folklore--Mali. 4. Cartoons and comics.] I. Title.

PZ8.1.E37 Su 2003
398.2'089'96345--dc21

2002026435

I AM THE
GREAT GRAY
ROCK
PAY ATTENTION
WHILE I TELL HOW
THE GREAT COUNTRY
MALI
CAME TO BE

3

IN THE BEGINNING THE BEASTS RULED ALL AFRICA

THEN PEOPLE CAME

AND THEY WANTED TO RULE.
BUT TO DO THIS, THEY HAD TO LEARN WHICH GHOSTS RULED THE LAND... WHICH WERE GOOD AND WHICH WERE EVIL.

SO BEFORE LONG THEY KNEW THE WAYS OF THE EARTH AND ITS BEASTS... AND FROM THEN ON, RULED THE BEASTS!

BUT THERE WAS A PLACE YET UNKNOWN TO SUMANGURU WHERE LONG AGO A GENTLE PEOPLE CAME FROM THE GREAT DESERT TO SETTLE. IT WAS A LAND OF TREES, HILLS AND GRAZING FOR CATTLE.

THEY CALLED THEIR PLACE MALI AND ENJOYED THE LEADERSHIP OF NARE FAMAKAN - A WISE AND NOBLE MAN.

QUIET!... LISTEN TO OUR LEADER, NARE FAMAKAN, HE IS WISE!

WE ARE A PROUD PEOPLE...AND ONE DAY WE WILL BE A GREAT NATION.

AND INDEED, BEFORE LONG, THE VILLAGES OF MALI BECAME WELL KNOWN AMONG THE TRADERS WHO VISITED OFTEN.
... ONE DAY SUMANGURU RECEIVED A TRADER.

WHAT NEWS DO YOU BRING FROM YOUR TRAVELS?

IN THE LAND OF MALI, TO THE NORTH LIVE A GENTLE PEOPLE, SIRE!

9

SO AS SUMANGURU'S WARRIORS ENTERED THE VALLEY THEY WERE MET BY ONLY HALF OF THE MALI.

...WHO PRETENDED TO FLEE WHILE SUMANGURU'S MEN PURSUED THEM INTO THE VALLEY...

WHERE THEY WERE ATTACKED FROM ABOVE.

THEY WERE TRAPPED

SUMANGURU'S BEST FIGHTERS TURNED AND FLED

OH, LOOK, SUMANGURU! THE MEN OF MALI ARE WINNING THE BATTLE!

15

16

NOW SUMANGURU BECAME MORE AND MORE POWERFUL!

DESTROYING THOSE WHO TRIED TO RESIST WITH HIS MAGIC.

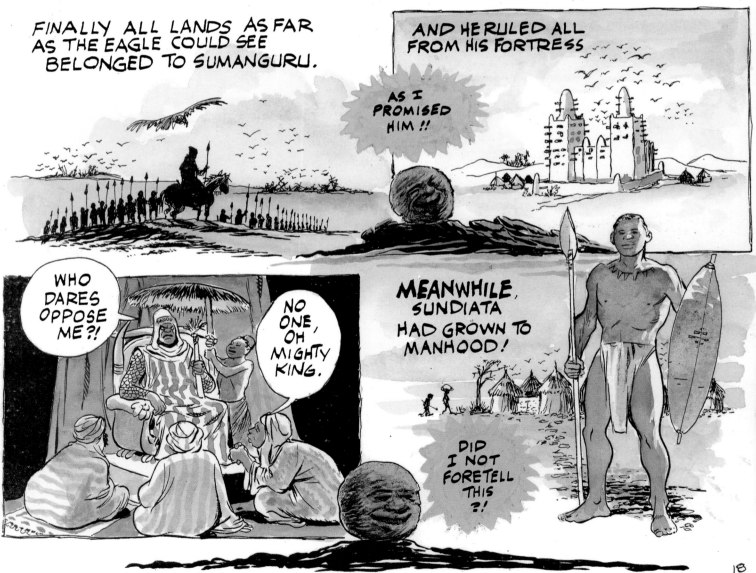

FINALLY ALL LANDS AS FAR AS THE EAGLE COULD SEE BELONGED TO SUMANGURU.

AS I PROMISED HIM !!

AND HE RULED ALL FROM HIS FORTRESS

WHO DARES OPPOSE ME ?!

NO ONE, OH MIGHTY KING.

MEANWHILE, SUNDIATA HAD GROWN TO MANHOOD!

DID I NOT FORETELL THIS ?!

19

31

AND IN THE YEARS THAT FOLLOWED,
MALI GREW INTO A GREAT COUNTRY

THERE, SUNDIATA REIGNED AS ITS LOVED
KING UNTIL HE WAS VERY OLD.

32